# English Language Arts

# K-2 ELA

## Volume 3

**Topics**
Consonant Digraphs
Nouns
Pronouns
Verbs

©2013 OnBoard Academics, Inc. All Rights Reserved

# K-2 ELA
# Volume 3

---

© 2013
OnBoard Academics, Inc
Newburyport, MA 01950
800-596-3175
www.onboardacademics.com

---

ALL RIGHTS RESERVED. This book contains material protected under International and Federal Copyright Laws and Treaties. Any unauthorized reprint or use of this material is prohibited. No part of this book may be reproduced or transmitted in any form or by any means, electronic or mechanical, including photocopying, recording, or by any information storage and retrieval system without express written permission from the author / publisher. The author grants teacher the right to print copies for their students. This is limited to students that the teacher teachers directly. This permission to print is strictly limited and under no circumstances can copies may be made for use by other teachers, parents or persons who are not students of the book's owner.

# Table of Contents

| | |
|---|---|
| **Consonant Digraphs** | **4** |
| Consonant Digraphs Quiz | 9 |
| **Nouns** | **10** |
| Nouns Quiz | 14 |
| **Pronoun** | **15** |
| Pronouns Quiz | 20 |
| **Verbs** | **21** |
| Verbs Quiz | 26 |
| **Adjectives** | **27** |
| Adjectives Quiz | 32 |

# OnBoard Academics Workbook

## K-2 ELA

# Consonant Digraphs

**Key Vocabulary**

consonant

digraph

# OnBoard Academics Workbook

**K-2 ELA**

**Digraphs**

Read each sentence and listen to the sound and notice the spelling of the consonant digraph.

Look at this shell, Mom.

It's phenomenal! Where did you find it?

At the beach.

A digraph: when two consonants come together to make one sound.

# OnBoard Academics Workbook

**K-2 ELA**

**Match and fill in the box each word containing a consonant digraph with the picture.**
Circle the consonant digraph.

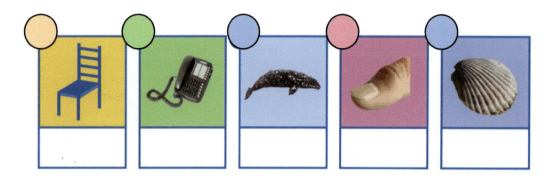

whale   thumb   shell   phone   chair
_____

**Highlight or circle the digraphs.**

 **Shelly collects shells.**

 **Charlie chews chocolates.**

 **Thor thinks he is thirsty.**

 **Whitney watches whales.**

 **Phil phones his friends.**

# OnBoard Academics Workbook

**K-2 ELA**

**Create words by connecting the boxes.**
On which side are the digraphs?
Write the words below.

# OnBoard Academics Workbook

## K-2 ELA

**Complete the paragraph by filling in the blanks with words containing digraphs. Fill in the boxes with words containing these beginning digraphs.**

Dad sat in a beach _____. It was too

hot, so he moved into the _____.

" _____ feels better," he said.

Mom took a _____ with her camera.

"I'll frame it _____ we get home,"

I said.

_____

| th | ch | ph |
|---|---|---|
|  |  |  |
|  |  |  |
|  |  |  |

| wh | sh |
|---|---|
|  |  |
|  |  |
|  |  |

OnBoard Academics, Inc.  www.onboardacademics.com

# OnBoard Academics Workbook  K-2 ELA

Name_____

## Consonant Digraphs Quiz

1. The word shape has a digraph.  True or false?

2. Circle the digraph that you can use to complete the sentence.  We had a __ __ at on the phone.
   a. ch
   b. th
   c. ph
   d. sh

3. Circle the digraph that you can use to complete the sentence. The child is __ __ ree years old.
   a. ch
   b. th
   c. ph
   d. sh

4. Circle the digraph that you can use to complete the sentence. __ __ o is coming over?
   a. Ch
   b. Th
   c. Wh
   d. Sh

OnBoard Academics, Inc.          www.onboardacademics.com          9

# OnBoard Academics Workbook

K-2 ELA

# Nouns

**Key Vocabulary**

person

place

thing

OnBoard Academics Workbook                K-2 ELA

**Nouns**
A noun is a person, place or thing.

**Sort the nouns.**

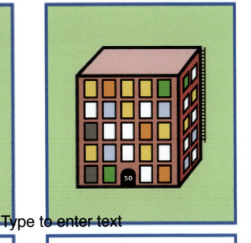

| person | place | thing |

---

| person | place | thing |
|---|---|---|
|  |  |  |
|  |  |  |
|  |  |  |

| pilot | teacher | principal |
| house | computer | apartment |
| ruler | book | ballpark |

# OnBoard Academics Workbook

K-2 ELA

**Can you think of some nouns for these three categories?**

| person | place | thing |
|---|---|---|
|  |  |  |
|  |  |  |
|  |  |  |

---

**Circle the nouns.**

> Twinkle, twinkle, little star,
>
> How I wonder what you are.
>
> Up above the world so high,
>
> Like a diamond in the sky.
>
> Twinkle, twinkle, little star,
>
> How I wonder what you are.

# OnBoard Academics Workbook

**K-2 ELA**

**Use the context of the paragraph to fill in the missing nouns.**
Suggestions are listed in blue boxes.

My _____ and I go to the same _____,

so we ride the _____ together.

The _____ thinks that we look alike and

sometimes gets our _____ mixed up.

Thankfully, this doesn't happen at _____!

| school | names | bus | home | hand |
| driver | room | dog | sister | cookie |

OnBoard Academics, Inc.   www.onboardacademics.com   13

# OnBoard Academics Workbook                K-2 ELA

Name_____

## Nouns Quiz

1. A noun is a person, place or thing.  True or false?

2. Circle the group of words containing only nouns.
   a. magazine, long, read
   b. big, computer, type
   c. swim, noisy, pool
   d. sand, beach, ocean

3. Most sentences have nouns.  True or false?

4. Fill in the blank.  My _____ has fleas.
   a. happy
   b. warm
   c. dog
   d. erasure

5. Fill in the blank. We saw a zebra in the _____.
   a. zoo
   b. supermarket
   c. farm
   d. treehouse

# OnBoard Academics Workbook  K-2 ELA

# Pronoun

**Key Vocabulary**

noun

pronoun

singular

plural

# OnBoard Academics Workbook

**I'm making a home movie!**
Fill in the blanks with pronouns.

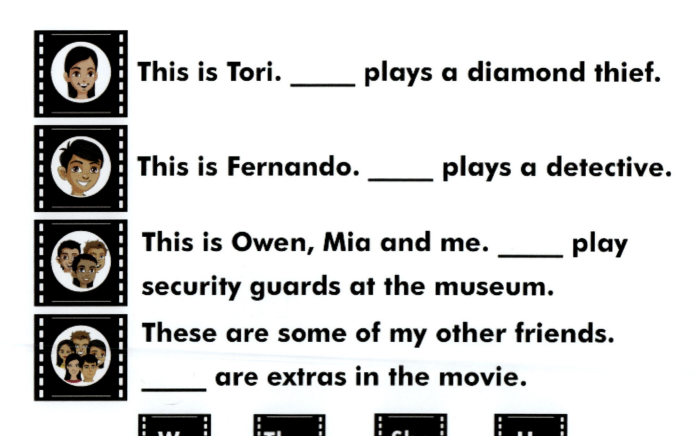

This is Tori. ____ plays a diamond thief.

This is Fernando. ____ plays a detective.

This is Owen, Mia and me. ____ play security guards at the museum.

These are some of my other friends. ____ are extras in the movie.

We   They   She   He

A pronoun takes the place of a noun.
Why do you think we use pronouns?

# OnBoard Academics Workbook

## K-2 ELA

**Pronoun or noun?**
Sort the words.

| pronouns | nouns |
|---|---|

| man | girl | it | they |
|---|---|---|---|
| she | he | puppy | friend |
| nurse | us | we | kitten |

OnBoard Academics, Inc.      www.onboardacademics.com

**Who is he?**

Alison and Owen were on a walk.
"Look at that bird over there," Alison said.
"Wow, that's so cool," he shouted.

Who is "he"?

**Owen**        **Alison**        **The bird**

_____

**Sort the words.**
Pronouns can be singular or they can be plural.

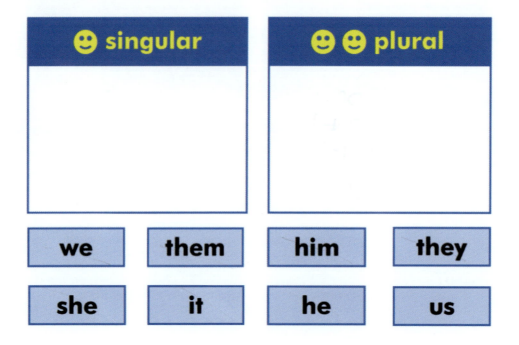

# OnBoard Academics Workbook

**K-2 ELA**

**Fill in the missing pronouns.**

My brother, Owen, plays on a baseball team called the Blues. _____ plays first base. My friend, Tori, is also on the team. _____ is a pitcher. _____ play every Saturday. My Dad and _____ have been to every game this season. _____ are the Blues' biggest fans!

**OnBoard Academics Workbook**         K-2 ELA

Name_____

## Pronouns Quiz

1.  A pronoun is an action word.  True or false?

2. Fill in the blank.  _____both have the same first
   name.
   a. He
   b. She
   c. It
   d. We

3. Fill in the blank. _____ are identical twins.
   a. Them
   b. They
   c. She
   d. It

4. Circle the singular pronouns.
   a. he
   b. they
   c. them
   d. we

# OnBoard Academics Workbook

K-2 ELA

# Verbs

**Key Vocabulary**

verb

noun

action word

OnBoard Academics Workbook  K-2 ELA

**Verbs**
Verbs are action words.

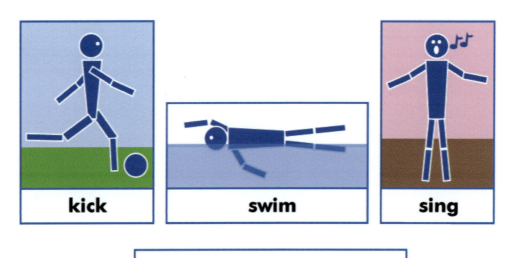

**Sort the words.**

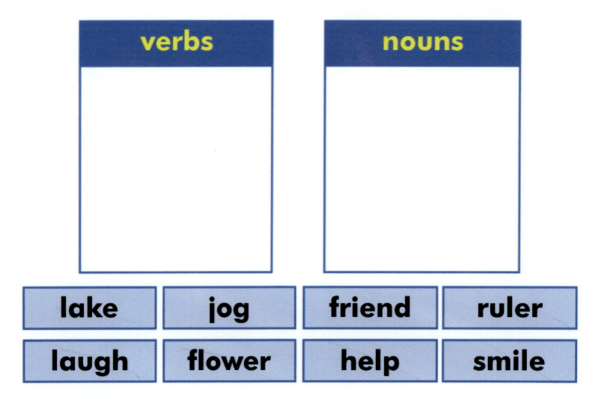

# OnBoard Academics Workbook

**K-2 ELA**

**Verbs at home and at school.**
Fill in the boxes with verbs that describe things you do at home and things you do at school.

**Highlight or circle the verbs.**

The itsy bitsy spider
Climbed up the water spout.
Down came the rain
And washed the spider out.
Out came the sun
And dried up all the rain,
And the itsy bitsy spider
Climbed up the spout again.

# OnBoard Academics Workbook

**K-2 ELA**

**Fill in the blanks with verbs.**
Use the suggestions in the yellow boxes.

Mia _____ to music in the evenings. Her brother, James, likes to _____ TV. Both of them like to _____ on the computer and to _____. Mia _____ her music player last week. James _____ it behind the sofa.

| play | read | lost | looked |
| played | found | watch | listens |

# OnBoard Academics Workbook

K-2 ELA

**Add your own verbs.**
Think of verbs for this text and fill in the blanks.

Mia likes to __*bake*__ cookies. James likes to _____ them! Last week, when she was _____ cookies, the telephone _____ . Mia was so busy _____ on the telephone that she _____ about the cookies, and they _____ . James didn't want to _____ any!

# OnBoard Academics Workbook       K-2 ELA

Name_____

## Verbs Quiz

1. A verb is a person, place or thing.  True or false?

2. Please _____ your hand if you want to speak.
   a. twist
   b. move
   c. wiggle
   d. raise

3. Mia _____ her cookies with James
   a. takes
   b. likes
   c. shares
   d. moves

4. Mom _____ her car.
   a. walked
   b. wished
   c. wrote
   d. washed

5. That joke made me _____.
   a. sleep
   b. cry
   c. laugh
   d. eat

# OnBoard Academics Workbook — K-2 ELA

# Adjectives

**Key Vocabulary**

adjectives

describing words

# OnBoard Academics Workbook

K-2 ELA

**Describe Javiér's hair.**

**Javiér has ☐ hair.**

**Long, black, spiky. What do we call these words?**

**What adjectives would you use to describe this dinosaur?**

_____
_____
_____
_____
_____
_____

# OnBoard Academics Workbook

K-2 ELA

**Dinosaur adjective word search.**

| a | g | h | m | i | v | e | k | d | v |
|---|---|---|---|---|---|---|---|---|---|
| s | g | h | u | n | g | r | y | d | x |
| u | v | u | w | l | o | i | k | d | s |
| o | r | g | t | k | d | b | n | k | c |
| i | c | e | q | u | m | i | g | o | a |
| c | k | f | e | h | o | u | r | u | r |
| o | e | s | b | l | v | y | k | d | y |
| r | n | f | d | h | o | p | g | u | t |
| e | c | k | b | k | c | i | d | o | t |
| f | c | g | f | t | b | i | y | o | t |

big

huge

scary

ferocious

hungry

OnBoard Academics Workbook　　　　　　　　K-2 ELA

**Think of adjectives that help us to describe pigs.**

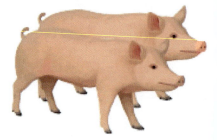

**1**　They have ___ skin.

**2**　They often have ___ tails.

**3**　They have ___ snouts and ___ eyes.

_____

**Think of adjectives that help us to describe sharks.**

**1**　Most types are ___ in color.

**2**　They often have ___ teeth.

**3**　The Great White is a ___ type.

OnBoard Academics, Inc.　　　www.onboardacademics.com　　　30

# OnBoard Academics Workbook  K-2 ELA

**Identify the adjectives.**
Highlight or circle the adjectives in this text.

Owen was excited. Today was his first day at a new school. He ate a large breakfast, grabbed his heavy backpack, and ran to catch the yellow school bus.

"Have a great day!" shouted his proud Mom and Dad.

_____

**Match the adjectives.**
These adjectives are across from the wrong nouns. Draw a line to pair them with a noun that makes more sense.

| adjective | noun |
|---|---|
| old | soda |
| smelly | nail |
| rusty | socks |
| cold | desk |
| tidy | painting |

OnBoard Academics, Inc.     www.onboardacademics.com

**OnBoard Academics Workbook**   K-2 ELA

Name_____

## Adjectives Quiz

1. An adjective is an action word.  True or false?

2. I have a _____ pillow.
   a. fruity
   b. fast
   c. fluffy
   d. friendly

3. The table had a _____ leg.
   a. wobbly
   b. painful
   c. cheerful
   d. anxious

4. The sun was _____ yellow.
   a. dark
   b. bright
   c. little
   d. fluffy

5. The ballerina wore a _____ outfit.
   a. old
   b. slow
   c. fancy
   d. cold

# OnBoard Academics Workbook     K-2 ELA

Newburyport, MA 01950

1-800-596-3175

OnBoard Academics employs teachers to make lessons for teachers! We create and publish a wide range of aligned lessons in math, science and ELA for use on most EdTech devices including whiteboard, tablets, computers and pdfs for printing.

All of our lessons are aligned to the common core, the Next Generation Science Standards and all state standards.

If you like our products please visit our website for information on individual lessons, teachers licenses, building licenses, district licenses and subscriptions.

Thank you for using OnBoard Academic products.

Printed in Great Britain
by Amazon